READING CORNER

Clever Lad

Written by
Justine Furminger

Illustrated by
Lisa Williams

W
FRANKLIN WATTS
LONDON•SYDNEY

Justine Furminger

"I love writing stories about animals and children. Children make me laugh, so my job as a teacher is brilliant!"

Lisa Williams

"I loved drawing the pictures for this book. I hope you enjoy reading it just as much!"

Lad is Lizzie's dog. He is big and black.

People say he can't do things.

Lad would not jump
like Rosa's dog.

He would not crawl

like Ravi's dog.

He would not beg

like Sally's dog.

He would not even howl
like Simon's dog.

9

But Lad did like to sniff.

One day, Lad sniffed his
way down the road.

13

He sniffed his way

across the park ...

... over the bridge ...

... and into a van!

Suddenly, the van began to move.

It went a long, long way.

When the van stopped, Lad got out. But he was lost!

19

Lad sniffed.

He sniffed again.

Then he started to run.

Lad jumped over fences.

He ran and ran across the fields.

Lad crawled under gates.

He begged for food outside houses.

He sniffed and sniffed until
he found his way home.

Lad howled under
Lizzie's window.

Lad is Lizzie's dog. He is big and black. People say he can't do things.

But Lizzie and Lad know better!

Notes for parents and teachers

READING CORNER has been structured to provide maximum support for new readers. The stories may be used by adults for sharing with young children. Primarily, however, the stories are designed for newly independent readers, whether they are reading these books in bed at night, or in the reading corner at school or in the library.

Starting to read alone can be a daunting prospect. **READING CORNER** helps by providing visual support and repeating words and phrases, while making reading enjoyable. These books will develop confidence in the new reader, and encourage a love of reading that will last a lifetime!

If you are reading this book with a child, here are a few tips:

1. Make reading fun! Choose a time to read when you and the child are relaxed and have time to share the story.

2. Encourage children to reread the story, and to retell the story in their own words, using the illustrations to remind them what has happened.

3. Give praise! Remember that small mistakes need not always be corrected.

READING CORNER covers three grades of early reading ability, with three levels at each grade. Each level has a certain number of words per story, indicated by the number of bars on the spine of the book, to allow you to choose the right book for a young reader:

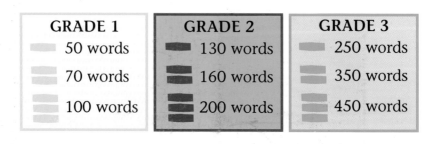

GRADE 1	GRADE 2	GRADE 3
50 words	130 words	250 words
70 words	160 words	350 words
100 words	200 words	450 words